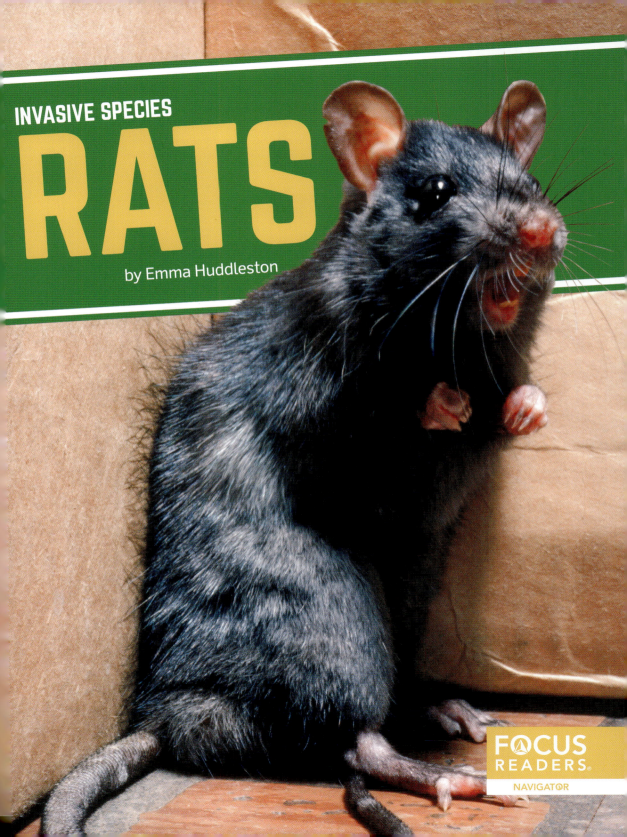

INVASIVE SPECIES

RATS

by Emma Huddleston

FOCUS READERS
NAVIGATOR

WWW.FOCUSREADERS.COM

Focus Readers is distributed by North Star Editions:
sales@northstareditions.com | 888-417-0195

Produced for Focus Readers by Red Line Editorial.

Content Consultant: Carrie J. Brown-Lima, Director, NY Invasive Species Research Institute; Atkinson Center for a Sustainable Future Faculty Fellow of Natural Resources, Cornell University

Photographs ©: Tom McHugh/Science Source, cover, 1; Shutterstock Images, 4–5, 8–9, 11, 16–17, 21, 27; iStockphoto, 7, 22–23, 28; Red Line Editorial, 13, 18; Ramakanta Dey/AP Images, 15; Megan Vick/WD4C, 25

Library of Congress Cataloging-in-Publication Data
Names: Huddleston, Emma, author.
Title: Rats / by Emma Huddleston.
Description: Lake Elmo, MN : Focus Readers, [2022] | Series: Invasive species | Includes
   index. | Audience: Grades 4-6
Identifiers: LCCN 2021003745 (print) | LCCN 2021003746 (ebook) | ISBN 9781644938577
   (hardcover) | ISBN 9781644939031 (paperback) | ISBN 9781644939499 (ebook) |
   ISBN 9781644939901 (pdf)
Subjects: LCSH: Rats--Juvenile literature. | Introduced mammals--Juvenile literature. | Pest
   introduction--Juvenile literature. | Nature--Effect of human beings on--Juvenile literature.
Classification: LCC QL737.R666 H83 2022 (print) | LCC QL737.R666 (ebook) | DDC
   599.35--dc23
LC record available at https://lccn.loc.gov/2021003745
LC ebook record available at https://lccn.loc.gov/2021003746

Printed in the United States of America
Mankato, MN
082021

ABOUT THE AUTHOR

Emma Huddleston enjoys being a children's book author. When she's not writing, she can be found reading or running outside. She lives in Minnesota with her husband.

TABLE OF CONTENTS

CHAPTER 1

ISLAND PROBLEM

Sparkling seawater surrounds the Chagos Archipelago in the Indian Ocean. Green trees and bright flowers cover this chain of islands. But a problem lurks below the treetops. Black rats scurry across the ground. They eat bird eggs. As a result, the bird **population** drops. When that happens, less bird waste flows into

Rats have lowered the number of birds on many islands in the Pacific and Indian Oceans, including the Chagos Archipelago.

the water. This waste helps aquatic plants grow. It helps corals grow, too. With less bird waste, the corals and plants don't grow as well. Local fish **species** need corals and plants for food. But the fish have fewer food sources, so they do not grow as large as they once did. By eating bird eggs, rats have changed the whole **ecosystem**.

Black rats are not **native** to the Chagos Islands. They are an **invasive species** there. People brought the rats to the islands by accident. In fact, humans have brought black rats around the world.

In addition, people have brought brown rats to new areas. For example, brown

The lesser noddy is one Chagos Archipelago bird species that has been impacted by black rats.

rats are an invasive species in many cities. Together, brown and black rats are some of the most harmful invasive species on Earth.

CHAPTER 2

BLACK AND BROWN RATS

Black rats are native to India and Pakistan. They live in a wide variety of **habitats**. Their homes include forests, wetlands, and grasslands. Brown rats are native to northeastern China and southeastern Russia. They are also native to Japan. In the wild, brown rats tend to live in forests.

Brown rats are most active at night.

Black rats are known for climbing. They often nest in treetops. In contrast, brown rats burrow. Sometimes they make tunnels and rooms underground. The rats store food in certain rooms. They use other rooms for sleeping.

EATING ANYTHING

Brown rats search high and low for food. They are able to eat a wide variety of things. For example, they hunt lizards, fish, and other small animals. They search through people's garbage. Sometimes they even raid kitchens. Scientists study some rats' stomachs after they die. That way, scientists can see what the rats ate. In one rat, scientists found more than 4,000 different items.

Black rats are often called ship rats because they spread around the world on boats.

Brown and black rats are not problems in their native habitats. Predators such as birds, cats, and snakes hunt them. These animals keep rat populations in check.

But people have helped spread black rats for thousands of years. By 3000 BCE, black rats were living among people in the Middle East. Cities and roads helped people bring rats to Europe. By the 1200s CE, black rats lived across Europe.

In the 1400s, black rats made their way onto ships. They traveled around the world with explorers, colonists, and traders. They hid in ship hulls, storage areas, and living areas. When the ships reached land, black rats settled in new areas. People brought them to Africa and the Americas. Black rats also reached many islands in the Pacific Ocean. Today, they live in more than 50 countries.

Similarly, brown rats spread throughout the world along with humans. Reports of brown rats in Europe began in the 1500s. Their presence across the continent is more certain by the early 1700s. Brown rats likely spread to the United States in the 1770s. They traveled on ships in boxes of grain. Now, they live in many cities.

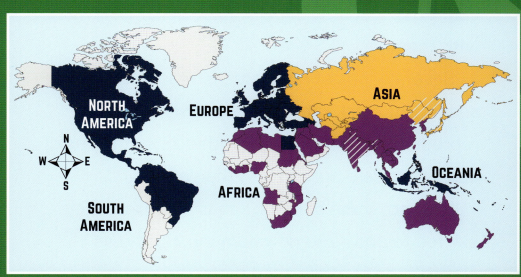

BLACK AND BROWN RATS AROUND THE WORLD

NORTH AMERICA

EUROPE

ASIA

OCEANIA

AFRICA

SOUTH AMERICA

 NATIVE BROWN RATS BLACK RATS BLACK AND BROWN RATS

POPULATION EXPLOSION

Every 48 years, black rats and bamboo plants each reproduce in huge numbers in northeast India. The two species have their massive reproductions at similar times. This event last happened in 2008. Bamboo plants released countless seeds. The forest floor became covered with them.

Several kinds of rats came to feast on the seeds. But black rats soon took over. They can reproduce much faster than other rats. Millions of black rats were born in less than a year.

Even so, some bamboo seeds survived. They started to grow into new bamboo. But those plants hadn't yet released their own seeds. So, huge numbers of rats still needed food.

A woman walks among flowering bamboo plants in Agartala, Tripura, a city in northeastern India.

They found farm crops. Many farmers lost all their crops. As a result, approximately one million people struggled to find enough food to eat.

Meanwhile, black rats had fewer babies. They saved energy that way. But when the seed explosion happens again in 2056, black rats will reproduce quickly.

CHAPTER 3

TROUBLE AROUND THE WORLD

Rats tend to take over new environments easily. One reason is that rats breed quickly. Black rats have three to ten babies at one time. Brown rats average eight babies at a time. And females can have multiple litters each year. Shelter, food, and warm weather allow them to breed more easily.

Brown rats eat up to one-third of their weight every day.

Another reason is that black and brown rats often have no major predators in non-native areas. When that happens, no animals slow their breeding. As a result, a pair of rats and their offspring could produce millions of babies in three years.

SPEEDY LIFE CYCLE

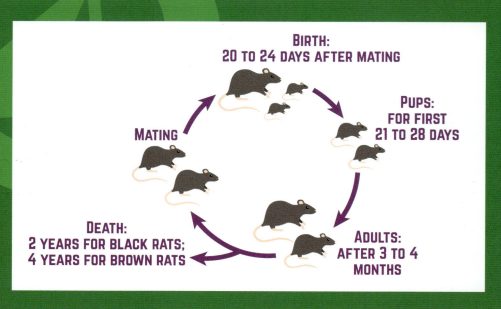

BIRTH: 20 TO 24 DAYS AFTER MATING

PUPS: FOR FIRST 21 TO 28 DAYS

ADULTS: AFTER 3 TO 4 MONTHS

DEATH: 2 YEARS FOR BLACK RATS; 4 YEARS FOR BROWN RATS

MATING

When rats take over an area, they can cause huge problems. For example, they carry bacteria and bugs on their bodies. Rats can spread disease to both humans and animals this way.

Black and brown rats threaten humans in other ways. Rats eat large amounts of people's food. In Asia, they eat enough rice every year to feed 200 million people. In Africa, rats eat approximately 15 percent of farm crops.

Rats are also invasive in cities. In New York City, brown rats thrive. Approximately two million rats live in the city. They raid trash bins for food. They live in sewers. They have even scared people by coming out of toilets in their homes.

However, rats mainly harm plants and other animals. Black rats slow or stop **pollination** by eating seeds and plants. In this way, they interrupt growing cycles of native plants. Rats hunt many kinds of

BLACK RAT TEMPLE

Many people hate rats for stealing food and spreading disease. But Rajasthan, India, has a temple for black rats. At the temple, rats are worshipped and sheltered. People believe the rats are the earthly bodies of a goddess. More than 20,000 rats live there. It may be the world's only temple dedicated to the animal.

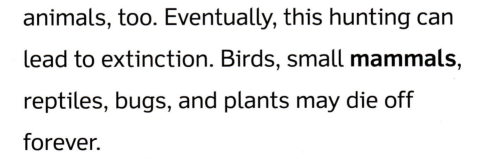

Black rats feast on milk in a temple for them in Rajasthan, India.

animals, too. Eventually, this hunting can lead to extinction. Birds, small **mammals**, reptiles, bugs, and plants may die off forever.

CHAPTER 4

GETTING RID OF RATS

Rats live nearly everywhere humans live. Getting rid of them is extremely hard. But it is possible on certain islands. For example, South Georgia Island is located near Antarctica. For 200 years, people brought brown rats to the island. Rat numbers grew. The island's native bird numbers dropped.

South Georgia Island is home to four kinds of albatross, some of Earth's largest flying birds.

In 2011, a British group took action. People dumped poison across the island. By 2018, the island was free of rats. Birds such as terns, albatrosses, and pintail ducks recovered.

People wanted to prevent new rats from reaching South Georgia. They learned that rats could only get there on ships. So, a group trained dogs to help. Dogs have a strong sense of smell. They can learn to sniff out rats. Dog experts work with the dogs. Together, they search boats. They remove the rats that the dogs find. That way, no rats reach the island.

Preventing the spread of rats is not just important for islands. It also helps

A trained dog sniffs around a boat to detect rats before the boat reaches South Georgia Island.

keep them out of people's homes. People avoid leaving garbage around. They keep food sealed up. Rats are less drawn to areas without sources of food. In homes and buildings, people seal their doors and windows. They fill cracks in walls or floors. These actions help keep rats out before they settle inside.

However, these methods do not help where rats have already spread. In those areas, people must work to remove rats. Traps and poison are two common

SAVING THE KIWI

Wellington, New Zealand, used poison and traps to get rid of black rats. People wanted to make a safe area for native birds, such as the flightless kiwi. As of 2017, New Zealand had helped clear more than 100 small islands of rats. People were still working to get rid of them on the country's larger islands.

New Zealand is the only place kiwis live.

ways to get rid of rats. People use other methods, too.

For example, New York City has one of the world's largest rat problems. Rats in the city thrive on huge amounts of trash.

New York City produces more trash than any other city on Earth.

The city's government tries to control the rats in several ways. City workers sometimes use blood thinners. They put the thinners in bait. When rats eat the bait, they bleed on the inside. They die after a few days. Many experts say this method is a necessary evil. Otherwise rats could cause a disease outbreak.

New York City uses less painful methods, too. Some city workers put frozen carbon dioxide in rat burrows. It turns into a gas. It seeps into the burrows. It causes rats to fall asleep and never wake up.

Scientists are also testing chemicals to stop rat breeding. St. Louis, Missouri, tried one of these chemicals in 2018. Workers put the chemical in bait. Rats ate it, and breeding slowed. With less breeding, the rats were easier to control.

Rats are still a major problem in many places around the world. They are likely here to stay. But people are working hard to control their numbers.

FOCUS ON
RATS

Write your answers on a separate piece of paper.

1. Write a sentence that describes the main ideas of Chapter 2.

2. Do you think people should kill invasive animals such as rats? Why or why not?

3. What place became free of rats in 2018?
> **A.** New Zealand
> **B.** South Georgia Island
> **C.** New York City

4. Why might using carbon dioxide be a less painful way of getting rid of rats than other methods?
> **A.** Carbon dioxide causes rats to fall asleep before they die.
> **B.** Carbon dioxide only causes rats to leave the area.
> **C.** Carbon dioxide only stops rats from having more babies.

Answer key on page 32.

GLOSSARY

ecosystem
A community of living things and how they interact with their surrounding environment.

habitats
The types of places where plants or animals normally grow or live.

invasive species
Plants or animals that people bring to a new place and that harm people, native plants, or native animals.

mammals
Animals that have hair and produce milk for their young.

native
Living or growing naturally in a particular region.

pollination
The process of spreading a fine powder made by plants to help them reproduce.

population
A group of animals living in a particular area.

species
A group of animals or plants that are alike and can breed with one another.

TO LEARN MORE

BOOKS

Gilles, Renae. *Invasive Species in Infographics*. Ann Arbor, MI: Cherry Lake Publishing, 2021.

Hand, Carol. *Controlling Invasive Species with Goats*. Minneapolis: Abdo Publishing, 2020.

Rodger, Ellen. *Backyard Dwellers*. New York: Crabtree Publishing, 2020.

NOTE TO EDUCATORS

Visit **www.focusreaders.com** to find lesson plans, activities, links, and other resources related to this title.

INDEX

Answer Key: **1.** Answers will vary; **2.** Answers will vary; **3.** B; **4.** A